Stand By Your Brand

Internet Branding Manual

Tonja Ayers

Stand By Your Brand

Copyright © 2013 by Tonja Ayers

First Printing March 2014

Stand By Your Brand
Emperial Publishing
P.O. Box 211194
Detroit, MI 48221-1194
(313) 449-8543
info@emperialpublishing.com
www.emperialpublishing.com

ISBN-13: 978-1496127754

ISBN-10: 1496127757

Cover design by twentytwomedia via Fiverr.com

Table of Contents

Introduction

My name is Tonja Ayers and I am a Retail Coach. I am an experienced business leader and have been an entrepreneur for almost 20 years. I have founded several businesses and The Shoe Lady, a women's retail shoe store which opened April 14, 2000 located in Detroit, Michigan has been my greatest success. My years of entrepreneurial experience combined with my training and education enables me to provide you with a wide array of information in the retail arena.

Foreword

Branding, as a whole, is crucial for any serious business as a company's brand is what differentiates it from its rivals. In today's computer age, it is essential for most businesses to have an internet presence to remain competitive. Effective online branding, simply like its offline counterpart, helps bring cognizance to your unique business by creating buyer demand.

I started my first shoe business in 1995 under the name of Secrets however my customers would address me as 'The Shoe Lady". Five years after opening, I changed the name to "The Shoe Lady'. I had a logo created, purchased a sign and had the logo painted on the outside. I ordered clothing and paraphernalia with 'The Shoe Lady' brand and became a walking billboard. I thought the transition to internet marketing would be easy because I had established my brand locally however it was quite the opposite.

In this book, I am providing you with valuable information on how to build your internet brand. Information which was not available to me when internet marketing was 'new'.

Chapter One – The Basics

Successful branding uses hi-tech tools to produce an internet presence for your business. Graphics and overall website design which reflect your company are a few of the significant factors necessary to bring your internet brand alive. A website that helps buyers easily and quickly find the info they need is the key to getting buyer interaction and eventually, business. Your branding plan ought to include great design factors and ease of utilization to produce an effective and efficient total impression.

A strong internet image will make the difference between a buyer who purchases from your website or switches to your rivals.

Remember, internet buyers can leave your site and go to your rivals at the click of a mouse. A great deal relies upon the impression they receive from your website. Branding seeks to convey a prompt unique message about your business to your target customers.

Chapter Two – The Beginning

Branding is much more than a simple logo, slogan or unique color scheme. Creating a logo or slogan are the initial steps however a strategic promotional and marketing plan must be developed to create a 'mental' thumbprint within your target market thus successfully branding your image.

Analyze the Rivalry

Among the keys to producing a successful brand image is to differentiate yourself from your rivalry. You will have to know how buyers see your rivalry.

You have to recognize how your rivals differentiate themselves from other people. In addition to that, you should know your rivals strengths and weaknesses. Your business may benefit from knowing this info by learning how to strategize your business from their weaknesses. You may use this knowledge to differentiate your company from your rival.

For example, if your business is a bakery and the closest bakery closes everyday for lunch from 2:00pm to 3:00pm, you may want to run a special during that hour to generate foot traffic to your store. If a competing website closes down a week for the holiday, you may want to step up your advertising the week before and offer a discount code to online shoppers. Use what you learn to your benefit.

Look Within

Now that you recognize your rivalry's strengths and weaknesses you are able to start to focus on your company's issues. Perform a SWOT analysis (Strengths, Weaknesses, Opportunities, and Threats), learn from it, and utilize it to your advantage.

After completing your analysis, begin to think of ways to successfully market to your customer base. Be creative and learn to think outside of the box. Don't be afraid to try something new because you've never heard of another business doing it. You may the first! Innovation is key.

Know Your Buyer

Learn more about the buyer. Know their buying behavior. How frequently do they buy?

Do they purchase only during sales or promotions? Do they purchase an array of products or services or simply a select few?

These are questions you should ask to better market to your buyers. In addition to that, know your buyer's lifestyles, needs, mentalities, and attitudes. Knowing and working with these personality traits are also key to marketing success.

During the years of running my shoe store, I realized lunch hours and after-work hours were my busiest time of day during the week. From this I learned all new inventory had to be on the floor before 11:00am for my lunch crowd and any mid-day deliveries needed to be out and available for purchase no later than 5:00pm.

Be Your Brand

Make certain your company truly represents what your brand identifies you with. For instance, if one of the traits your brand identifies your company with is politeness, be polite. This means every employee from the receptionist all the way up to the CEO has to live by your brand.

Don't be afraid to wear your brand. I have attracted many customers due to conversations which initiated from wearing t-shirts, watches, etc with 'The Shoe Lady' logo displayed on it.

Chapter Three – Be an Expert

Demonstrating yourself as an authority in your field will help you acquire both recognition and respect. Believe it or not, that same recognition and respect transfers immediately to your company. If individuals trust that you truly recognize what you're talking about, they'll feel great about investing in your product.

A website is the best place to begin. Construct a professional looking website with sound and informative material and you'll have a source of authority information to direct buyers to.

Remember that it's beneficial to give

away some of your treasured knowledge free of charge. Provide the buyer something of value up front and they'll label you as a legitimate source to go to for whatsoever your company might offer.

Article marketing is a particularly effective technique to accomplish that authority status as it gives you the power to distribute a small number of articles to a vast number of content-rich sites. The more places your name pops up, the more individuals will be exposed to your website and product.

A different way to demonstrate your expertise is through internet forums and blogs. This is a bit more casual than article composition. It allows you to remain in the first person and talk candidly with interested internet surfers. The conversational tone utilized in such settings will put more potential buyers at ease.

Not only will they view you as an authority, they'll likewise feel connected to you as a real human being. In addition to that, such places provide buyers the chance to ask questions and give you the opportunity to back up your product in the face of critique.

Discover the correct places to gain recognition. Put yourself out there and command respect through that exposure. Spotlight your accomplishments and successes. Branding yourself as an authority is all about getting other individuals to realize something about you that you already recognize.

Chapter Four - Representation

Your website should have a logical look and feel to every page. If a visitor travels to additional pages and they look different, they might believe they unexpectedly left your website and then leave it all together.

Icons for going back or to the next page, and even the icons that line your menu should follow the same theme as your website as part of your marketing endeavor. Every aspect of your site ought to be about your brand. Standing out from the rest isn't nearly as important as having other people recognize your website.

An easy concept for internet market

branding is your logo as an icon. You might then utilize this as buttons and every time an individual has to click, your logo makes an imprint. Obviously it will have to be much smaller than the main logo on your page or additional areas to be utilized as a menu icon, perhaps as small as 16 x 16 pixels, but the reduced image will continue your branding throughout your pages and offer an advantage to your marketing effort.

In addition, with this level of branding throughout your website there will be no doubt in your visitor's mind where they are. You might even make it so a visitor bookmarking your web site will see the icon in his or her favorites, further imprinting the image. Remember, returning visitors frequently purchase more than first time visitors and keeping your image in their brains will aid your marketing efforts.

With a bit of creative branding, prospective customers will automatically think of you when they see your logo. This is among the simplest yet most effective branding techniques.

Have you ever considered the significance of color in branding? Color plays a vast role in memory recall. It excites all the senses, instantly conveying a message like no other communication technique.

Selecting the right dominant color for your brand is important. This color should appear on all your promotional material. The following list details the most common impression each color conveys:

Blue: Cool blue is sensed as trustworthy, dependable, fiscally responsible and secure. Blue is a particularly popular color with financial institutions.

Red: Red sparks off your pituitary gland, increasing your pulse rate and causing you to breathe more rapidly. Count on red to arouse a passionate response.

Green: Green connotes health, freshness and serenity. Deeper greens are affiliated with wealth or prestige, while light greens are calming.

Yellow: In most societies, yellow is affiliated with the sun. It communicates optimism, light and warmth. Particular shades seem to motivate and stimulate originative thought and energy. The eye sees bright yellows before any other color, making them good for point-of-purchase displays.

Purple: Purple is a color favored by originative types. It evokes mystery, sophistication, spirituality and royalty. Lavender evokes nostalgia and sentimentality.

Pink: Hot pinks express energy, youthfulness, fun and excitement. Dusty pinks seem sentimental. Lighter pinks are more romantic.

Orange: Cheerful orange arouses exuberance, fun and vitality. Orange is deemed gregarious and frequently childlike. Lighter shades appeal to an upscale market. Peach tones work well with health care, restaurants and beauty salons.

Brown: This earthy color transmits simplicity, durability and stability. Particular shades of brown, like terracotta, might convey an upscale look.

Black: Black is sober, bold, powerful and classic. It produces drama and connotes sophistication. Black works well for expensive products, but might also make a product look heavy.

White: White implies simplicity, cleanliness and purity. The human eye views white as a brilliant color, so it at once catches the eye in signage. White is frequently used with infant and health-related products.

Chapter Five – Selling With Branding

What comes to mind when you think of the Coca Cola brand? Does an image of a red can with words Coca Cola written in white show in your mind's eye, or maybe a coke bottle? Pick your niche on the net and brand your name accordingly. Be known for excelling in one area before moving on to the next project. Coca Cola concentrated on building the Coke brand for 75 years before introducing Sprite. I'm not saying you have to wait that long but surely you get my point. You don't want to confuse your customer by trying to establish your brand with too many concepts.

Suggestions:

1) A website or blog.

2) Opt In box. Set up an option for website visitors to join your email list. This is an inexpensive, quick and effective way to contact your customer base.

3) Photo & Signature. Scan a groomed, smiling photo of yourself and your a written signature. This adds that individual touch to let your audience know you are a true person.

4) Audio and/or Video. Do you have a nice speaking voice? If so, mix this with your photograph and signature to humanize your site and institute rapport with your audience. You can do this by adding a mp3 file or a video.

5) Blog. A blog may be an add-on to your main site or be utilized as a free alternative to a site, at least till you're generating profits. You are able to combine every aspect of name branding mentioned in the above points into your free blog. Update your blog at steady consistent intervals with material specific to your vision. Refrain from writing about off topic material so as to keep your message and theme uniform. One way to keep your readers posted about your material is to use RSS feeds.

6) A Domain name. You are able to register a domain name and forward it to your blog. Utilize the domain masking feature that lets your site have a professional appearance.

Conclusion

If your internet marketing material provokes a picture in your brain that's simply not you, then most likely you have modeled your approach after someone else. If you hired someone to create your brand, make sure they get to know you by sharing your thoughts, and interjecting your personality into the content.

The answer to this dilemma is to be yourself and let your personality show through in your internet marketing content.

If you're writing a blog entry in the midst of a blizzard and it's "a bit nippy outside" don't hesitate to say so. If you let your personality shine your image will be your own, not one you've crafted that will alter daily depending on what you've read most recently.

There's lots of discussion on branding in regard to internet marketing. The basics of branding are to determine the picture you wish to portray and what message you wish to drive home.

While a few individuals may write a book on how to brand your business, there are truly only a handful of elements to consider - your image, your intent and your message. The intent of a brand is to craft something that will stick in the minds of individuals and help them to recall your business.

Producing and building a strong brand doesn't have to compromise your personality and should never compromise your integrity. The only true decision is whether you wish to be casual or professional. In the world of internet marketing, retaining your personality and your individuality will go far in branding your business. You'll be a lot happier with the long term results of your branding efforts if you don't attempt to be somebody you're not. Be yourself. Why die a copy when you were born an original?

Branding Tips

Your brand identifies you to your clients and seeks to engage them in an ongoing relationship. It represents the sum of all your marketing efforts and strategies — your logo, emails, advertisements, social media channels, and marketing.

Good corporate branding draws in clients, builds loyalty among those clients, and separates you from your competition. Your branding strategy should serve to attract the best business to your company. These are seven reasons a better brand can help your business this year.

1. Better branding helps you identify your target audience.

Many businesses make the mistake of assuming everyone is their target audience. These companies water down their brand while trying to please everyone and they end up attracting no one. Nothing sets them apart.

A strong branding strategy develops and uses an ideal client profile to define a niche market. Then, all messages target that niche. This will improve lead generation because you target the right audience, rather than simply a large audience.

2. A consistent brand will attract clients consistently.

When thinking of branding, take a look at Proctor & Gamble. This company consistently attracts its target market — moms — to its brands because of brand consistency. The more your brand is recognized through your website, materials, and even your email signature, the more a client will see you as a solid market leader.

3. Strong brands turn even small businesses into empires.

Yes, image is everything especially with today's savvy consumers. They can spot a sloppy logo or slapped together website in seconds. Better branding elevates your company from a "mom and pop" operation to a business worthy of a second look.

4. Branding strategies hone your message to meet your client needs.

Too often, marketing messages are focused only on what marketers want to say rather than what clients want to hear. A strong brand strategy examines client needs, addresses them, and anticipates those needs. By demonstrating a commitment to serving clients, you will build a loyal following and turn current clients into brand advocates.

5. Set yourself apart in a crowded marketplace.

There is a lot of competition out there and you need to set yourself apart. A strong brand strategy separates you from the competition by highlighting what you do differently and how you operate as a thought leader in the industry.

6. Branding focuses your efforts.

Spending time developing a strong brand strategy helps your company develop focus on your core mission and focuses all efforts directly on achieving those key goals. A weak brand has lost sight of that mission and can lead efforts astray.

7. Strong brands save time and money.

A lack of a branding strategy can cause you to lose out on potential business opportunities while you spend time trying to educate clients on who you are. Start off this year with a strong brand strategy and hit the ground running so you can put your efforts into growing your business.

Your brand is your strongest asset to build lead generation, attract and retain top clients, and drive traffic to your website. Start working with a better brand strategy and see the results for your business.

Courtesy: www.under30ceo.com